A gift from
Robert Fussell

In memory of

Ike Scott

PUTTING MY WAY

PUTTING MY WAY

A Lifetime's Worth
of Tips from Golf's
All-Time Greatest

JACK NICKLAUS
with KEN BOWDEN

Illustrations by Jim McQueen

WILEY

John Wiley & Sons, Inc.

Published by John Wiley & Sons, Inc., Hoboken, New Jersey
Published simultaneously in Canada

Portions of chapter 1 are reprinted with the permission of Simon & Schuster, Inc., from *My Story* by Jack Nicklaus with Ken Bowden. Copyright © 1997 by Jack Nicklaus.

For general information about our other products and services, please contact our Customer Care Department within the United States at (800) 762-2974, outside the United States at (317) 572-3993 or fax (317) 572-4002.

Wiley also publishes its books in a variety of electronic formats. Some content that appears in print may not be available in electronic books. For more information about Wiley products, visit our web site at www.wiley.com.

Library of Congress Cataloging-in-Publication Data:

Nicklaus, Jack.
    Putting my way: a lifetime's worth of tips from golf's all-time greatest / Jack Nicklaus, with Ken Bowden.
        p. cm.
    ISBN 978-0-470-48779-2 (cloth)
    1. Putting (Golf) I. Bowden, Ken. II. Title.
    GV979.P8N54 2009
    796.352'35—dc22

                                                                                2009006810

Printed in the United States of America
10 9 8 7 6 5 4 3 2 1

For all of those who would enjoy the greatest game of all
so much more if only they could putt better.

Contents

Preface

Figuring roughly, golf is a game played half through the air and half along the ground. To a greater or lesser degree, recovery from mistakes is always possible within the first half, but less so and eventually never so within the second.

Miss a makeable putt and the hard fact is that it's a stroke gone forever.

That would seem to suggest that the number of books about rolling the ball across greens should at least equal those about flying it to and from fairways. In fact, the reverse is the case. Golf book bibliographies show that a great many more texts have been published about how to swing the clubs that hit shots through the air than about rolling the ball into the hole.

The reason, I assume, is that the tee-to-green game is perceived as golf's more challenging, exciting, and difficult-to-master element. Trouble is, without the other half—the putting part—we simply don't have a game.

Accordingly, when my friend and longtime collaborator, Ken Bowden, suggested that we should round out our literary efforts at a dozen volumes with a book containing pretty much everything I've learned about putting, the idea intrigued me. And especially in regard to the format he proposed.

All but one of my "how-to" books include some degree of advice on the gentle art of rolling a 1.68-inch-diameter ball into a 4¼-inch-diameter hole. However, their structures are such that for a reader to track down all of that material—even if he or she possessed or could get access to every volume— would require a tedious amount of digging through more than a foot-high stack of volumes.

"So how about," suggested Ken, "gathering together and organizing the best of all that material into one volume as our final instructional?"

When he added that, by a rough count, I had published something like five hundred items on just about every conceivable aspect of putting during my playing career, I became even more interested. Finally, Ken clinched the project with his assurance that the best of that material could be updated and organized for presentation in mostly short and self-contained passages, while covering every element of golf's "second act" in an appropriate sequence.

In substance, therefore, if rarely the exact same wording, everything herein has been published previously, although never in the coherent order of a single volume. Also, most of that information and advice has been either consolidated or amplified with new material, to provide everything I've learned about putting in a logical and orderly format.

Approximately half of the items deal with the physical elements of rolling the ball effectively—I hate to use the word "mechanical" in relation to putting—with the other half focused on the mental and temperamental aspects of getting the ball in the hole in the least number of strokes.

It has always seemed to me that putting is by far and away the most neglected element of golf at the game's recreational levels in every aspect—attitude, strategy, technique, instruction, practice . . . you name it.

Hopefully, *Putting My Way* will help mitigate that situation.

What I can definitely assure you is that, if you learn how to knock 'em in more easily and more often, your enjoyment of the game will grow proportionately.

1

ATTITUDE

First, a Little Philosophy

Par allows for two putts per hole, and, as par is mostly 72, that means putting theoretically is half the game. In actuality, it's a little less than that for both tour players and the majority of amateurs, the former because they average less than two putts per hole, and the latter because they take proportionately more strokes reaching greens.

Either way, though, putting has a bigger impact on scoring than most golfers are inclined to admit to themselves. It's an overstatement to say the tours are nothing more than putting contests, but it's equally true that, if you can't get the ball in the hole, you won't be much of a contestant on any of them. And I guess that's true, too, of all those weekend Nassaus.

> Putting has a bigger impact on scoring than most golfers are inclined to admit to themselves.

Attitudes toward putting among both golfers and nongolfers are interesting. They range all the way from Ben Hogan's conviction that rolling the ball along the ground was not really golf, to Bobby Locke's assertion that putting is the most critical part of the game. (Possibly those views had something to do with the fact that putting was the weakest element of Ben's play and the strongest part of Bobby's.)

I guess the in-between attitude is nicely typified by a high-handicapper friend of mine after following me in a tournament in Florida years ago. That day I hit every fairway and green in regulation or better, and had the ball within a dozen feet of the cup eight or nine times, yet could score no better than a 68.

"Boy," said my pal afterward, "that must have been frustrating. If you *only could have putted,* you'd have shot 62 or 63."

If I only could have putted . . . ? Well, I made five birdies by holing sizable putts, and three-putted only once from a difficult position. But, to my average-golfer friend, all that was by the way. What struck him hardest was not how fortunate I had been on those five birdie putts, but how "unlucky" I had been not to make five or six more.

And this mind-set explained to me why he himself was such an awful putter.

His expectations were simply way too high.

At tournaments with many nongolfers or occasional players in the galleries, you can tell from the stunned silence when you miss anything under about 20 feet that a lot of people have unrealistic ideas about the difficulty of rolling a 1.68-inch-diameter ball into a 4¼-inch-diameter hole over a surface of tightly mown but always slightly irregular grass. They just can't see what can be so difficult about something that looks so easy. Powder a drive way out there but into the weeds and many of those folks will "Oooh" and "Aaah" and shout "Yeah!" and

"Wowee!" Miss from six feet and some will look at you as though you should be in a padded cell.

What's even more intriguing is how even the best putters have a tough time looking upon this facet of the game realistically, particularly in regard to their own ability at it.

The best putter I ever encountered was Arnold Palmer in the late 1950s and 1960s. To this day, however, there is no way Arnie would concede that he was ever more than just decent on the greens. Whenever I've tried to tell him differently, his response has always been, "Boy, if I could have putted only *half* as well as *you* did . . ."

I guess the reason Arnold is so hard on himself about putting is that, during his best years, when to everyone else he seemed to hole everything he looked at, he came to see great putting as never missing. If that's true, then he has lots of company among tour golfers. In all the years I was out there, I can't remember one player—myself included—admitting that he was a "great" putter and not many who would go along even with "very good."

My late friend Gardner Dickinson, who admitted after his retirement from competition that he lost tournaments purely as a result of convincing himself he was not a good putter, believed ego or "macho" played a big part in this syndrome. Whereas, he explained, it's manly to crush out huge drives, hit towering

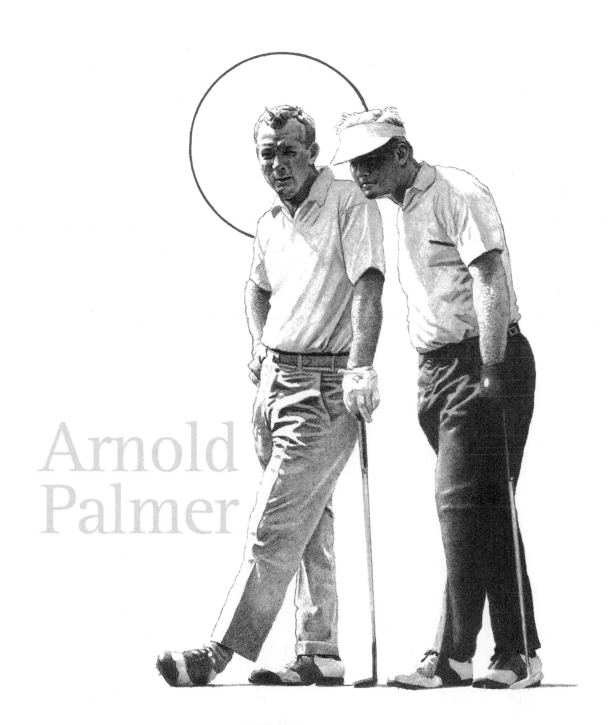

Arnold
Palmer

long-irons, and spin wedges tight to the pin, it's somehow a bit nerdy or wimpy to be good at rolling the ball along the ground into a hole.

Whatever the truth of the "I-can't-really-putt" mind-set, the truth is, of course, that just to obtain, then hold on to, a tour card a golfer has to be an excellent putter. To win consistently, he has to rank—by *realistic* standards—much of the time in the "great putter" category.

What, then, makes us all so reluctant to admit such skills? I think Gardner's reasoning has some validity, but there are other factors as well.

I know from my own experience that, the better a golfer putts, the better he *expects* to putt, until, like Arnie at his peak, it can become inconceivable to him that he should ever miss. In other words, the greater one's success, the harder it becomes to accept the realities of the difficulty of putting and the luck factors involved in it—as illustrated by even a putting machine missing two or three times from a distance of 10 or so feet.

Another reason for the reluctance to admit skill with the short stick may be the seemingly overwhelming significance of putting in winning and losing at golf. I am sure there are players on the tour now, as there were in my time, who believe they never would lose if only they could putt all the time like whomever currently heads the putting stats. That is obviously baloney. But yet it is also understandable that a guy whose living depends on birdies and eagles would equate his achievements primarily with his performance on the greens.

And, of course, the Mount Everest in that regard is how hard it is to get your mind past the fact that putting is the one element of the game where, unlike a missed drive or approach, a miss is a mistake from which you cannot recover.

Or, in short, a stroke gone forever.

The biggest lesson I have learned from all of this is that putting is the element of golf that rears up and bites you hardest when you try to *force* success.

There have been occasions when consciousness of putting's *finality* made me too conservative on the greens, defensive when I should have been aggressive, and some of those times cost me dearly. But there have been even more times when such awareness made me try to force the ball into the hole, and all that happened was that I got even more frustrated because it wouldn't go, until eventually I was caught up in that vicious circle of ever-increasing self-imposed pressure I described a moment ago.

The essence of putting to me, then, is that it is far more difficult, and much more dependent on luck than most of us can easily either grasp or accept, but that the better we become able to do so, the less risk we run of having it sabotage our entire game.

Positiveness Pays Big-Time

Putting at times will always frustrate you, as it has every golfer throughout history. Nevertheless, if you want to score your best at golf every time out, do not allow that or any other negative emotion to provoke you into discounting or disliking that part of the game, compared to hitting the ball from tee to green.

The great Ben Hogan allowed himself to do that despite his high intelligence and immense self-discipline, and in my view it contributed to him rarely putting as well as he played from tee to green, especially as he aged.

Obvious as it may sound, I suspect many recreational players don't realize—or accept—how absolutely essential a sound and repeatable method of stroking the ball is in order to score well, and thus never work hard enough on that part of the game to develop one.

believe

To help rectify this, recognize that when you lack confidence about *how* you're going to hit a putt, you'll have even less about *where* the ball is going to finish.

So never neglect working on that stroke—and on *believing*

in it. Practicing putting may not be as much fun as pounding drivers on the range, but the payoff will be far greater.

What should help you do that work is recognizing that, although putting can be the most frustrating element of golf, it is actually the easiest to master in physical terms.

Proper Planning Breeds Confidence

If you believe you can get the ball in the hole, a lot of the time you will, even if your technique appears to be unorthodox or even downright faulty. If you don't believe you can get the ball in the hole, most of the time you won't, even though your technique may seem flawless. Which is one reason I was never able in tournament play to putt until was 100 percent "ready," by which I mean I had convinced myself I could make any putt I regarded as of realistic holeable distance.

More than anything else, proper planning breeds confidence.

The first planning requirement in reading greens is judging very accurately at what speed and along what path the ball must roll to reach and fall in the hole. Therefore, always carefully evaluate every factor that will influence how the ball will behave—turf condition, break, grade, grain, and moisture are primary in determining speed and line.

Regarding grain—the most neglected of those factors by amateurs—if you had played all over the United States you would know that the grass in Florida grows toward the setting sun, in California toward the ocean, and in most other parts of the country toward the nearest water or away from mountains. You would know that when a bent or Bermuda grass green looks light and shiny the grain is with you, and when it looks dull or dirty the grain is against you.

If you believe you can get the ball in the hole, a lot of the time you will, even if your technique appears to be unorthodox or even faulty.

The second confidence requirement is the ability to aim the ball where you've decided it should go. This is mechanical, a matter of proper setup alignment that can be learned and mastered by anyone who will give sufficient time and thought to the task.

The third confidence requirement is the ability to repeatedly stroke the ball in a way that transmits a feeling of fluid, yet solid, contact from the clubface to your hands. This is partly mechanics, and it is also influenced by the tempo and rhythm of your stroke. But it is mainly a matter of what I can only call instinctive "touch." Some people seem to be born with fine "touch"—I think I was blessed with a reasonable share. But, if you don't have it naturally, the only way you're going to get some is through knowledge of and mastery of technique.

The fourth requirement is absolutely no second-guessing— which means believing that you have made a sound plan and always sticking to it as you set up to and stroke the ball.

You will never, of course, make 'em all whatever you do. Apply these four basics, however, and you will make a lot more.

Golf's Most Easily Mastered Skill

I've gotten the impression from all the pro-ams I've played that quite a few recreational golfers acquire a Ben Hogan–like deep-seated feeling that rolling the ball along the ground is not a rational part of the game's challenge compared to hitting it through the air.

The negativity deriving from such a mind-set can be a killer, especially in terms of making the effort necessary to mastering putting's special psychological and physical challenges.

What should help such players become more positive about putting is recognizing that, although it will at times be the most frustrating element of their golf, it is actually the easiest part of the game to master in physical terms.

Applying Sufficient Attention

To inspire you to putt positively, recognize and accept that, no matter how well you hit the ball from tee to green, your score won't reflect those shot-making skills unless you also roll the ball into the hole in as few strokes as possible. Conversely, no matter now badly you hit the ball through the air, by putting skillfully you will always save something in terms of your overall score.

Even though they may sound self-evident, never lose sight of those two facts if you want to be a winning player.

Indeed, it was with them in mind that long ago I built a putting green in my backyard to remind and encourage me—although doing so was often less "fun" than range work—to continue attending to my putting skills as much as the other departments of my game.

And it surely paid off, because, looking back, I would say that in at least half of my best rounds, my tee-to-green golf wasn't especially brilliant. I missed too many fairways or failed to hit a lot of approaches close to the flag, plus other slips. But many times I managed to cancel that out by pitching and chipping adroitly.

Plus, even more often and importantly, by sinking a half-dozen or so putts I wouldn't normally have holed.

Believe in Yourself

To me, good putting, particularly under pressure, is much more a matter of mental approach than physical skill—although mental approach will never overcome poor greens-reading or stroking ability. *

I may not have been a great putter "mechanically," but, most of the time when I needed to be, I believe I was mentally stronger than average with the putter in hand. For instance, some players, when the vise tightens, will tell themselves, "Oh, gosh, if I miss this putt, I'll drop back a shot," or something similar. My messages to myself were always along the lines of, "I need this putt to stay ahead or stay within reach, *So go ahead and knock it right in!*"

You might have the prettiest stroke in the world, but to be a really good putter you absolutely have to believe that you're going to make 'em. And that mentality becomes more critical the more under the gun you find yourself.

> To me, good putting is much more a matter of mental approach than physical skill.

I almost always was able to convince myself that I was going to make the putts that really mattered, in which the major factors were willpower and sheer competitiveness—as also exemplified by my wife, Barbara.

Although we have never gotten out on the golf course much together, I'll forever remember one nine holes that we did play.

Barbara's greatest asset in tennis, her best game, was competitiveness—and, boy, did it come through that time at golf!

Just about every time she hit the ball with the putter it went in the hole. And she did it with an awkward stance, faulty alignment, a spread grip with her right thumb off the shaft, and a fast backswing followed by a jerky forward stroke on which her head bobbed up as the blade bounced off the turf before striking the ball.

Such can be putting! Two percent technique; ninety-eight percent desire and determination.

Inspiration First, Mechanics Second

Following on from that, it would be fair to say that—although never quite to Barbara's extent!—putting has been the least "grooved" or "mechanized" part of my game. Beyond a few personal keys, mainly related to alignment and tempo, my adamant beliefs about sticking to time-proven fundamentals on full swing technique went out the window the moment I walked onto a green.

Don't get me wrong here about intensity of effort.

I would do just about anything to make putts drop. I would vary my setup or stroke, not only from day to day but sometimes from hole to hole, or even from putt to putt. Obviously some of those changes were dictated by course conditions, such as green contour or speed. But the majority were purely "method" adjustments: a searching and experimenting for a certain alignment, or a particular stroking pattern, or a quality of tempo and "feel"—and especially those last two.

Again, don't get the impression from this that I lacked confidence in my putting fundamentals. The adjustments were always small. But there's no doubt the reason for this constant fiddling around was that I really do believe that great putting is much more inspirational than mechanical. Or, in short, if you believe that making some small change will help you get the ball in the hole more often, it quite likely will.

That's why it still tickles me after all these years to recall the number of times just the smallest adjustment in some aspect of setup or stroking made all the difference.

Value Knowledgeable Advice

Unconsciously, over a period of time ahead of the 1967 U.S. Open at Baltusrol, I had let my putting stroke get longer and longer. This eventually resulted in me unknowingly slowing the clubhead down as it approached the ball, which you flat must not do with *any* golf shot.

Two evenings before the Open began, a friend of mine from the tour, watching me frustratedly stroke practice putts, suddenly said, "Jack, why don't you go back to the way you used to putt years ago? You know, take it back a little shorter then hit it harder."

Right there, I began to take a very short backswing and rap in putts from everywhere. The next day I sank them all in a practice-round 62. I felt like I couldn't miss, and I continued to roll the ball extremely well throughout the championship, three-putting only three greens while one-putting seventeen. Indeed, of the five shots I figured I had hit to win, four were putts.

Lesson: When someone who knows both *the* game and *your* game offers you a tip, listen hard.

Why Short Putts Are So "Pressurized"

It doesn't take much technique to roll a 1.68-inch-diameter ball along a smooth and level surface into, or into the immediate vicinity of, a 4¼-inch-diameter hole. With no pressure on you, you could do it one-handed most of the time. But there is *always* pressure on the shorter putts, even when you're just goofing around on the course alone.

One reason is that you feel you should always make the shorties, which, when score matters and others are watching, produces a psychological fear of appearing inept and embarrassing yourself should you miss.

As I stressed earlier—and can't do again too strongly—an even bigger reason is that you instinctively, if not consciously, recognize that any theoretically easily "makeable" putt is golf's "last chance" shot. While you still have a chance to recover from all other missed strokes, the pressure escalates from knowing, consciously or otherwise, that to miss a "tiddler" is to lose a stroke forever.

Accordingly, it seems to me that most near-"gimme" putts are missed less through faulty technique per se than the effects of a negative attitude, headed by flat-out fear. And the only answer to that—assuming sound technique, of course—is willpower and determination.

Accepting Golf's Imperfectibility

Accordingly, my policy any time I missed a "makeable" putt in tournament play was always to spend a minimum amount of time and psychic energy berating myself, and a maximum amount of effort switching my mind to what came next. Sure, I needed that putt. Sure, I could have read it better, stroked it better, willed it into the hole harder.

But no one's perfect. I missed it. And life goes on.

And here comes another tee, another hole, another challenge . . .

Accordingly, I tried to do the only thing that really makes sense in competitive terms, which was to erase what had just happened from my mind as quickly as possible to make maximum room for what was coming up next.

In which regard, knowing and accepting that golf has been imperfectible for every player in the game's history—and always will be—can at least help you move on without letting anger or frustration destroy the entire round.

2

THE PUTTER

Finding the Right One

The odds are fairly long against your putter being the culprit if you have only spasmodic trouble on the greens, but if you become consistently inferior in this phase of the game then a change of putter might provide at least a psychological boost.

Of course, it could do much more than that if the putter you've been using hasn't fully suited either your stroking style or the type of greens you normally play.

For instance, if your natural or preferred putting motion is a long, flowing stroke, you'll probably be most comfortable and effective with a fairly heavy club, and perhaps also with a slightly longer than standard shaft.

If, on the other hand, you're more of a rap or tap putter, you'll likely do best with a medium-weight or even lighter club. Certainly, the faster the greens, the more control a lot of good players feel they get from a reasonably light putter.

If you're in doubt about your present putter, I suggest you ask your pro to let you try a few clubs from his rack—ideally while having him look over your putting action.

Belief that you've got the right club in your hands is as important as believing that you know how to use it.

Also, don't discount going to a "belly" or an even longer putter if you've never tried one. I never felt the need to do so, but in recent years quite a few tour players have successfully changed to one or the other, in some cases permanently and others periodically. If you go that way, however, recognize that different techniques are involved that will most likely require some intensive practice.

Whatever club you use, belief that you've got the right club in your hands is as important as believing that you know how to use it.

Weight Change Requires Caution

Although I know of players carrying different-weight putters for fast and slow greens, it's never appealed to me.

In my book, it's difficult enough adjusting to unfamiliar putting surfaces without also having to adjust to a change in putter "feel."

By all means use a light putter if you play primarily on fast greens, or a heavier-headed one if you play mostly on slow greens. But if you are a golfer who likes to travel to many different courses, I suggest you find yourself a medium-weight putter that is "right" for you in every other respect, then stick with it.

Knowing "Sweet Spot" Critical

Before you obtain a new putter, it's important to locate the "sweet spot" to be sure it's where you want it to be, because the farther away from that point you contact putts, the fewer you will hole.

You can find the "sweet spot" easily by bouncing a ball along the putter face while holding the club vertically in front of you by the shaft with its face horizontal. When you feel no twisting or vibration in the shaft, the ball is bouncing on the "sweet spot."

I like a putter with its "sweet spot" right in the center of the blade, because that's where I instinctively will tend to strike the ball, and where consciously I try to do so. But you'll find that some putters have their "sweet spot" located closer to the heel, so you may have to do some searching.

Incidentally, identifying the "sweet spot" with a mark on top of the blade—as I did with a filed line on my "best" putter (see next item)—helps most players contact the ball more solidly more often.

Match Lie to Stroking Style

"Feel" should always be the final arbiter in your selection of a putter.

Beyond that, there are no hard-and-fast rules about what constitutes a good putter, any more than there are about what constitutes a good putting method. So, if a club feels good and gets the job done, stick with it, whether it's the newest-fangled thing on the market or you dug it out of Uncle Ernie's attic.

Here, to me, is the most important "technical" factor in choosing a putter: whatever the style, it must place your hands in a comfortable as opposed to a contrived position when soled flat behind the ball.

Thus, if you putt best with an upright method, that is, with your hands high—the style of most good putters on tour these days does seem to be fairly upright—then get a putter with an upright lie. But if you perform best with a flatter stroke, match the lie of your putter to that lower-handed method.

However, if a putter seems just "made for you" in every way except its lie, consider having your pro simply bend the shaft or hosel to produce the necessary angle.

My "Best" Putter

At the 1959 Walker Cup at Muirfield in Scotland, I bought a lightheaded, hickory-shafted Ben Sayers blade putter in the nearby town of North Berwick that I used for the rest of my amateur career, finding that it served me well on the mostly fast bent-grass greens used for top amateur tournaments.

Tour course greens now are mostly excellent, but back when I turned pro in 1962 many were poor to mediocre, thinly grassed and bumpy or overgrassed and deadly slow—sometimes even newly aerified and/or top-dressed. The result was that, by the time I got to my fifth event, I'd become almost certain that the Ben Sayers putter—although excellent in every other way—was too light for such surfaces.

That was when George Low, a professional renowned for his putting ability—he was also quite a "character" who would bet on himself against any tour pro on practice greens and usually collect—asked me if I'd like to try one of the models he'd come up with under his "Sportsman" label. I quickly agreed, and George took me in the golf shop where he handed me one of his original Wizard 600 flanged-blade models. Using it, I shot 64 to tie for first in a pro-am, then tied for second in the tournament proper, and continued to putt better and better as the season progressed.

Although eventually I used a variety of other types of putters, looking back I have no doubt that that Wizard 600—not least because it was a couple of ounces heavier than my Ben Sayers—contributed more to my record than any other single club.

3

GRIPPING

How I Hold My Putter

Because my putting stroke is primarily a right-handed action, I want as much as possible of that hand on the club. Accordingly, I favor a reverse-overlap grip, meaning the forefinger of my left hand lays over the fingers of the right.

reverse–overlap grip

Another reason I like this grip is that it helps me to place my right hand directly behind the shaft with the palm parallel to the putterface, so that when I push my right hand squarely toward the hole, the putterface must also move in that direction.

Yet another reason I prefer the reverse-overlap grip is that, after using it for so many years, it feels supremely comfortable—and physical comfort over the ball in putting is imperative.

I hold the club in the same place on the shaft for all putts, but my grip pressure varies depending on the type of stroke I am using. Generally, you could describe it as easy to firm—never loose and certainly not tight.

I hold the putter predominantly in my fingers, with both thumbs set directly down the top of the grip. I seek a firmness in the pressure of my left thumb on the top of the club that I feel helps to create a center point or fulcrum for the stroke.

The back of my left hand is turned to face a little left of target, which helps prevent any tendency to turn the club in that direction on the forward swing and thus pull the ball.

Back in my rookie year on tour, I got a putting lesson related to my right-hand positioning from Jackie Burke Jr. that contributed to my career probably as much as any other single tip I received after turning pro.

Jackie
Burke

The 1956 Masters and PGA champion, Jackie was widely renowned for his putting ability and savvy, and, while playing a practice round with him ahead of my second pro tournament, I mentioned how erratic I had been on the greens in my first outing and asked what he thought.

Jackie told me my problem derived mostly from trying to pull the putterhead through the ball with my fingers, instead of pushing it through with the palm of my right hand.

He suggested that resetting my right hand so that the thumb was directly on top of the shaft and the palm directly beneath it would help a lot, and he was correct. I began to feel better on the greens as soon as I made the change, and it is a technique that I have stayed with ever since.

He suggested that resetting my right hand so that the thumb was directly on top of the shaft and the palm directly beneath it would help a lot.

Thanks again, Jackie!

My chief "touch" finger is my right forefinger, which I curl onto the club in such a way that its middle knuckle points down centrally between my heels. This is a safeguard against pushing or pulling the ball off-line with a finger that contributes much to the hitting. If my right forefinger was wrapped on the club so that its knuckle pointed toward the outside of my right heel, I'd tend to pull the ball; if it pointed to my left heel, I'd push putts.

There are a zillion ways to hold a putter. I don't think it matters much which one a golfer adopts, so long as it is comfortable, promotes a square-bladed swing through the ball, and is conducive to smooth stroking rhythm.

And, of course, that it gets the ball in the hole.

The Master Hand

I've often been asked, which should be the master hand in putting?

As with so many golfing questions, the answer has to be, "That depends . . ."

A lot of the finest modern putters on tour seem to feel that the left or leading hand should be in command of the stroke, but others insist that the right or trailing hand is the key performer.

As noted several times herein, fundamental to my putting has always been that my left hand *guides* the stroke while my right *pushes* the putterhead through the ball.

I believe many good putters over the years have felt similar hand roles to mine.

Top Grip Pressure Goal: Fluidity of Motion

To me, the most important consideration in putting is *consistent fluidity* of stroke, and grip firmness has major influence on that.

Accordingly, I've always tried to hold the putter sufficiently firmly to be able to control its head's path and face alignment during the stroke, but never so tightly that it can't swing naturally of its own weight and momentum.

I should add that, in the pursuit of consistency, I try to employ the same grip pressure on all lengths and types of putts.

If you sense that excessive, insufficient, or fluctuating grip pressure is hurting your putting, you need to experiment in practice to determine exactly what "strength" of grip works best for you, then stick with it.

In which regard, my observations in pro-ams over the years suggest that far more amateurs grip their putters too tightly than hold them too loosely. Another common fault—and an absolute killer—is varying grip pressure *during* the stroke, whether it be from loose to tight or vice versa.

4

SETTING UP

Three Absolute Essentials

I don't think the particulars of how you set up to or address putts matters much, so long as it allows you to meet three absolute essentials.

To putt effectively, you must first feel totally comfortable over the ball, which to me mostly requires being solidly balanced and physically stable. That's because awkwardness or discomfort in the setup almost invariably inhibits smoothness of stroking, among other important factors.

Y ou must
look down
vertically on the
starting line of
every putt

Second, you must look down vertically on the starting line of every putt—meaning that your eyes are positioned directly *above* the putt's starting line rather than to its inside or outside.

Eyes beyond the line and you will tend to pull putts left; eyes inside the line and you will likely push putts right. To check this factor, first assume your usual head position over the ball, then take one hand from the club and, with it, drop another ball straight down from the bridge of your nose. To minimize movement, hold the test ball in your teeth until the transfer.

Third, your setup should encourage and help you keep your head and body absolutely *motionless* throughout the stroking action. This I achieve most easily with a sense that I am set up sufficiently *behind* the ball to be striking it *away* from me. Thus, on almost all putts, I address the ball opposite my left toe or instep, then position my head low and well behind it. This provides me with the additional benefits of being able to see the part of the ball that I intend to strike, its rear, along with some if not all of my starting line. However, my "head well down and back" setup is a personal preference, and you should position your head wherever you are most easily able to keep it and your body stock-still while stroking.

In terms of body positioning, as previously noted, I would quite often slightly vary some element even during a tournament round, in search of either greater comfort or better balance

over the ball. Basically, I got my best results from what I felt was a reasonably "square" alignment of my feet and body with the starting line of each putt.

However, I don't believe the "mechanics" of the putting stance a golfer takes matter a darn so long as they provide those three essentials: comfort, stability, and correct eye positioning over the ball.

Ball Position Relative to Feet

Ball position at address in relation to the feet is important only in the sense that you should locate the ball where you can best swing the putterhead through it both squarely and low enough to the ground to meet the center of its face solidly.

For me, that position has normally been opposite my left big toe or instep.

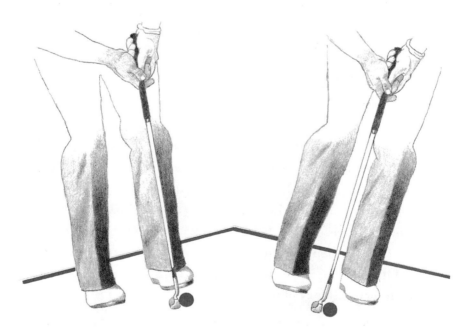

Putting severely uphill, I might move the ball forward a little, and back a little putting sharply downhill. But for you my positions might not be ideal, so this is an area in which you should experiment to discover what works most consistently well.

Shaft Angling

A few fine putters lay the club's shaft slightly back, with their hands behind its face at address, then return to that position at impact. It can be an effective way to get the ball rolling quickly—so long as you don't "thin" or even top it!

Other players angle the shaft slightly forward with the hands ahead of the clubface at address and impact, either in setting up or through a slight forward press with the wrists to initiate the stroke. That promotes solid contact via a slightly downward blow, but, since the ball tends to be driven into the green's surface, it may skid or otherwise react erratically if overdone.

My preference has always been to set the shaft perpendicular, or inclined very slightly targetward, with my left hand directly over the ball, then try to return to that position at impact.

That's because, over the years, I've found this produces the greatest consistency of roll.

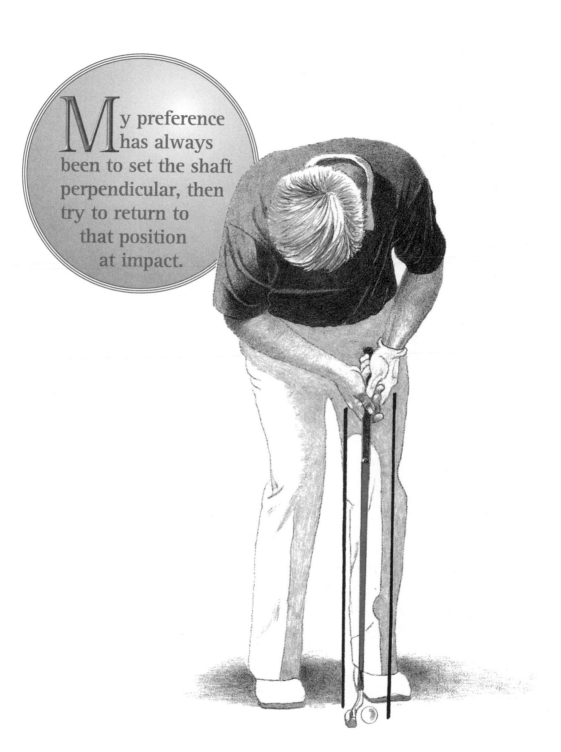

My preference has always been to set the shaft perpendicular, then try to return to that position at impact.

Stillness-Promoting Stance Adjustments

Setting up to putts feeling uncomfortable is an almost guaranteed way to ensure some part of you moves during the stroke that shouldn't, diminishing your chances of contacting the ball solidly and accurately with the putter blade's "sweet spot."

Sometimes, however, simply willing oneself to "stay still" doesn't get the job done, including for me.

When that has happened, I've sometimes licked the problem by making a conscious effort to set my weight on the *insides* of my feet or the *balls* of my feet. Also, addressing the ball with the feeling that my left heel is carrying slightly more of my weight than normal has sometimes saved the situation.

I call all three adjustments "anchoring" myself over the ball, and they have rarely failed to reinforce my overall feeling of stability at address.

Give them a try, and discover how hard it then becomes to sway.

anchoring

5

STROKING

My Stroke in Detail

The basic components of my putting stroke have generally remained pretty consistent over the years.

As an amateur I was a fairly stiff-wristed putter, but, as I began to play a greater variety of courses after turning professional, I found I could not consistently make solid contact with the ball with this rather "wooden" method. Increasingly, I felt I lacked "touch," and thus went for a while to the other extreme—an all-wrist stroke. Before long, however, that was modified into the combination wrist-arm type of stroking I used for most of my professional career.

Arm putters generally take the club back with the left hand in command, then hit the ball with the right hand. Like most wrist or wrist-and-arm putters, I take the club back with my right hand and also hit the ball with that hand. Meanwhile, the left hand acts primarily as a guide to steady and stabilize the stroke, while also serving as a sort of fulcrum for the hinging of the wrists.

Visualizing my right forearm working like a piston is an image that helps me greatly in using my right hand correctly throughout the stroke.

Visualizing my right forearm working like a piston is an image that helps me greatly in using my right hand correctly throughout the stroke. To "see," set up for, then sense that pistonlike motion, I need to bend far enough over the ball to position my right forearm horizontal to the ground, or close to that alignment. My setup also requires positioning the palm of my right hand so that it "looks" squarely at the starting line of the putt.

GREAT MEMORIES

Jim McQueen

Strive for "Gentle" Hands

I've always putted best with a distinct sense of gentleness in my hands, both in preparing for the stroke and executing it. Those feelings seem to produce a more consistent roll, which for me is critical to fine putting.

Visualizing the puttershaft as being extremely limber—as flexible as a length of rope or even a delicate glass rod—helps greatly in that regard. That's because the only way to swing the clubhead smoothly with such images in mind is very softly and evenly.

A very light grip initially helps achieve both goals, along with retaining finger softness throughout the action—no "grabbing" once the putter's in motion, always a fatal move.

When to Take a Tip

My putting had deteriorated after winning the 1980 U.S. Open, but playing with son Jackie prior to the PGA Championship a couple of months later he thought he spotted the problem: breaking off the stroke by stopping my hands and the putterhead at the ball. His suggested fix: swing my hands and the putterhead *through* rather than to the ball for what at first would feel an exaggerated distance.

We worked hard on it for a few days, and by the time we got to Oak Hill I was putting well enough to win my fifth PGA by seven strokes.

Moral: always take a tip from someone who really knows your game.

Jim McQueen

A Perfect Strike at
a Perfect Time

On a magical Sunday at Augusta National, I'd played the previous eight holes with a bogey and a par, but also four birdies and an eagle. Here at 17, after a poor drive I managed to cut a risky low-hit pitching wedge 120 yards to the green, where, thanks to heavy spin, it settled 11 feet from the hole. One more birdie, I figured, and I'd have a remarkable chance to win.

Obviously, the pressure was immense, but I've always thrived on pressure—especially in majors. Son Jackie—who was caddying for me—helped me read the slightly uphill putt, after which I managed a perfect stroke.

When the ball dropped, I led by one, and a little later, at age forty-six, had won my sixth Masters and twentieth major championship, if one includes my two U.S. Amateurs.

Jim McQueen

Jim McQueen

The Gentle Art of Starting Back

As we've discussed a number of times herein, a putted ball always slides or skids a little before beginning to roll. Nevertheless, imagination or not, I believe I putt best when I feel I'm rolling the ball truly end over end from the get-go.

Intensifying that sense, in my case, requires keeping the putterhead close to the ground, even though that increases the risk of stubbing it starting back.

My solution is obtaining both a physical sense and a mental picture of what I call "unweighting" the putter before I begin the stroke, by lifting its head very slightly off the ground.

A definite plus of this technique for me is that, by helping to keep my body very still, I am able to initiate the backswing more slowly and deliberately.

Look Hard, Remember Clearly

Careful observation and a good memory will help you putt better.

As an example, at the 17th hole of the 1959 Amateur Championship, I left myself, after a number of poor shots, with a 25-footer for a halve to stay one up against a tough opponent who'd just completed an effortless par.

Examining my putt from every perspective, I recalled that the grass on that particular green was a little lusher and thus had played slower than the others all week. Accordingly, I decided to stroke the putt more firmly; first, because it was a do-or-die effort, and second, because that would be more in accord with my gushing adrenaline.

Reminding myself to swing longer rather than produce a stroke-distorting harder hit to get the necessary distance, and after taking a few calming deep breaths, I canned the monster right in the heart, closed out my opponent, and reached my first national championship final.

Jim McQueen

Jim McQueen

One of My Toughest

I discussed this in the text, but am so proud of the moment I couldn't resist having it illustrated and repeating the story.

At the 17th hole in the fourth round of the 1962 U.S. Open at Oakmont, tied with Arnold Palmer, I faced one of the toughest putts I can recall—a 4-footer with first a break to the left, then almost at the hole a sharp curve to the right, and just super-scary fast all the way. I needed to make this terrifying little "tap-in" (ha!) to stay tied with Arn.

Not sure my pumping pulse and adrenaline flow would let me read both breaks and the speed correctly, after much study I decided my best policy was to hit the ball really hard—hard enough to eradicate both breaks and the question of pace by really ramming it into the hole.

The greatest dangers with such a strategy are, first, rushing the stroke, and second, moving one's body during it. Fighting both, I took a ton of time setting up, eventually fired hard, then with immense relief watched the ball whang against the back of the hole and plunk to its bottom.

Unforgettable!

Another repeat, I'm afraid, but again so joyful a moment I couldn't resist it being pictured.

This is perhaps the best-remembered putt I ever holed—from 40 feet off a slightly heavy 5-iron tee shot on the 16th green at the 1975 Masters.

I'll never forget how scarily close the hole was cut to the front plateau in the back right corner of the green. I watched very closely how my playing partner, Tom Watson's, ball rolled as it climbed the slope, but my main thought—with Tom Weiskopf and Johnny Miller chasing me so hard right behind—was, "Get close and make par." That was because leaving oneself a 3- or 4-footer on a green that slick under the kind of pressure I was under was an unbearable thought.

Then, straightening up after one last look, it occurred to me I could "see" the line as clearly as I ever had on a putt of such length, and my thought as I completed my setup became, *"Make it!"*

My stroke felt perfect, and, as the ball got to within about a dozen feet of the cup, I just knew there was no way it could miss and lifted my putter high overhead.

Then, as the ball dropped, our excitement was such that my caddie, Willie Peterson, and I turned into what one writer described as Indian war dancers, leaping around all over the lot.

Half an hour later I'd won a then-record fifth Masters.

Jim McQueen

Putting Starts at the Tee

For me, putting has always started at the tee, in determining, first, where ideally I want to place the ball on the green relative to its difficulty and most threatening hazards, then—if I'm playing more than a par 3—from where, off the drive, I can most easily achieve that goal.

The painting here illustrates a simple example of this process. Drive left and both fairway bunkers—plus, on the approach shot especially, the left greenside bunker—become threatening. Drive too far right and rough, trees, and the right greenside bunker represent a threat.

My safest driving zone therefore becomes the right half of the fairway, ideally with a club that won't reach the hazards if I happen to miss the shot left.

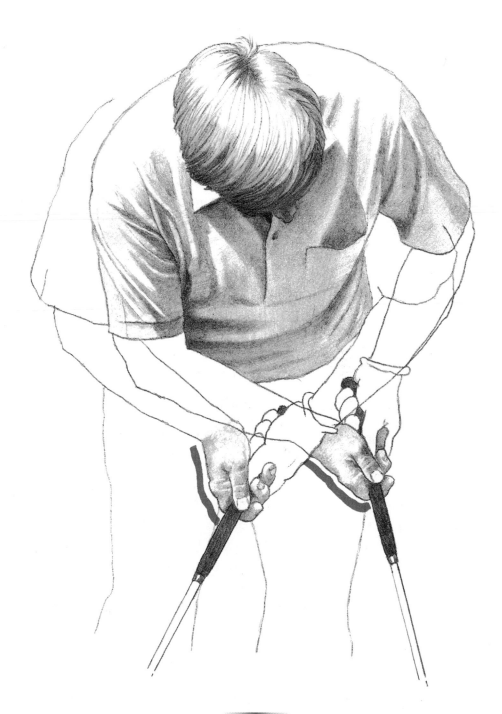

Since my putter shaft is vertical or almost so at address, I can swing it on short and medium-length putts pretty much along the target line throughout the stroke—meaning straight back and through. The longer the putt, of course, the more the clubhead must move inside the target line on the backswing, then inside again in the follow-through.

I do not make any conscious effort to keep the clubhead low to the ground on the backswing—although I don't "pick it up," either—but I do strive to keep it low and on line going out and after the ball.

As I have said and written a great many times over the years, and repeatedly herein, my overriding objective in putting is to develop a feeling of fluidity yet firmness at impact between my hands and the clubface, which tells me I am striking the ball accurately and solidly. The key to this sensation lies far less in the mechanics of the stroke than in its tempo.

Accordingly, for the sake of tempo more than anything else, I belong to the stroking rather than to the "rapping" or "popping" school of putting technique. My objective is not to "hit" the ball but to swing the putter back with my wrists and forearms at a relatively slow and deliberate tempo, then swing it *through* the ball at *exactly the same tempo* with reciprocating wrist-forearm motion.

The length of the backswing being the factor that primarily

controls the force of my stroke, I am particularly concerned about matching backswing size relative to the distance I want to roll the ball.

One final point that probably needs clarification in relation to my emphasis on the function of my right hand in the stroke is that, although that hand does most of the work, the left must always work in total harmony with it, particularly on the through-stroke. Also, if the left hand checks or quits at any point before impact, it will have a blocking effect on the right hand's action that will disrupt the swing path, the clubface alignment, or both.

Clubface Alignment Variations

I remember once writing way back that I was a "square to square" putter. Since then I learned the advantages of using different types of strokes for different moods and situations. Accordingly, in later years I was sometimes a square-to-square putter, sometimes an open-to-closed putter, and sometimes a closed-to-open putter.

Indeed, in 1972 I recall winning seven times—including the Masters and U.S. Open—using three different patterns of stroke. But I couldn't have predicted which it would be until I got to the tournament venues and checked out the green conditions.

What are the mechanical differences between those strokes? Well, really they are very slight.

When putting what I visualize as square-to-square, I endeavor to swing the club away from and back through the ball without any rotation of its face. When putting open-to-closed—which I've usually reserved for poor or slow or heavily grained greens—I allow the clubface to rotate slightly clockwise on the backswing and commensurately counterclockwise through the ball. (If the greens are very bad, I'll combine this open-to-closed action with striking the upper half of the ball, to produce extra overspin.) My closed-to-open stroke is simply the reverse of the open-to-closed action, the clubface rotating a little counterclockwise going back and commensurately clockwise going through, producing a soft or gentle sort of impact.

This is subtle stuff, of course, and I don't intend that the recreational golfer immediately try to adopt such methods. My recommendation to him is to stick with a square-to-square-type stroke until he has mastered the art of consistently striking the ball solidly on the putter's "sweet spot."

I describe my own variations simply to emphasize that whatever produces the necessary "touch" or "feel" is so much more the key to fine putting than any single element of mechanics.

"Touch" Matters Most, No Matter How

Never believe a fellow who wins an important tournament and then tells the world he wasn't stroking the ball worth a darn. Only a few of golf's big winners over the centuries may have been *great* putters, but be assured that anyone who finishes first at the top of the game is an *extremely good* putter, if only on particular occasions.

Yet the fact remains that, when you look back over putting styles, you find massive variations in methods. Indeed, in my time few of the greats seem to have putted the same way, at least by "mechanical" measure.

For instance, Lee Trevino, Billy Casper, and Bob Charles—three of my heyday's greens titans—putted entirely differently

from one another. Lee employed his wrists and forearms to produce a flowing stroking action. Billy picked the clubhead up with a wrist break rather than an arm swing and "popped" the ball into the hole. Bob putted stiff-wristed, swinging the club primarily from his shoulder sockets with his arms forming a virtually unchanging triangle. And, of course, I surely had my nose closer to the ground with a putter in hand than any of my peers!

The one thing all of us—and all the other fine putters in history—had in common was "touch," which, as the first item in this section emphasizes, always has been, is presently, and always will be putting's most critical element. But I also believe that none of the greats found their superb "touch" through "mechanizing" a stroke, nor do I believe they could have retained it that way. When I saw them out on the practice greens before or after tournaments, I never got the impression that they were trying to "groove" anything mechanical. Rather, I sensed they were seeking to heighten their sense of "touch," by constantly slightly adjusting and modifying the various elements of their setup, stroke, and—most of all—the *rhythm* or *flow* of their action.

So far as "touch" is concerned, it matters not whether you become a wrist putter or an arm putter or a shoulder putter, or use an overlapping or an interlocking or a left-hand-low or a "claw" grip.

What is critical is to discover then master whatever combination of putting's great many mechanical options produces the best greens "feel" for you personally, and then essentially stick with them.

Switching radically back and forth from round to round or day to day—or, even worse, as I've seen in pro-ams, from hole to hole or even from putt to putt—is sure to produce heartache.

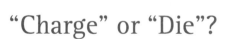

"Charge" or "Die"?

Rather than drive yourself crazy with mechanics, you will develop and retain "touch" most easily having determined whether you are temperamentally basically a "charge" or "die" putter, then sticking with whichever approach you decide upon.

Arnold Palmer in his early years was the greatest "charge" putter of my time, and perhaps of all time. Arnie's goal on putts that he decided were makeable—which meant virtually all of them—was to hit the back of the hole hard and true enough to "trap" the ball into the cup.

Experiment with both approaches, then make your choice and stick with it.

Which, of course, is fine when it's working well, but can be tough on the nerves, as well as the score, when a player is even slightly "off" for whatever reason.

I have been essentially a "die" putter throughout my career, because I came to believe early on that it offered better percentages in terms of developing and sustaining "touch."

Accordingly, my aim on most of what I regard as makeable putts is to roll the ball gently just over the front edge of the cup when I stroke it perfectly, or topple it in from one side or the other when I don't.

Experiment with both approaches, then make your choice and stick with it.

Forward Pressing

Forward pressing to initiate the putting stroke is of course optional, but the more trouble you have starting the putterhead back smoothly, the more it might help you.

Whereas the forward press used for tee and approach shots involves a combination of hand and body motions, forward pressing in putting requires only a slight and gentle movement of the hands toward the hole via a slight targetward inclination of the wrists, from which the backswing is a slow, smooth recoil.

The biggest risk with this way of initiating the stroke, of course, is that it has a tendency to open the putterface slightly. So if you use the technique, be careful about overdoing it.

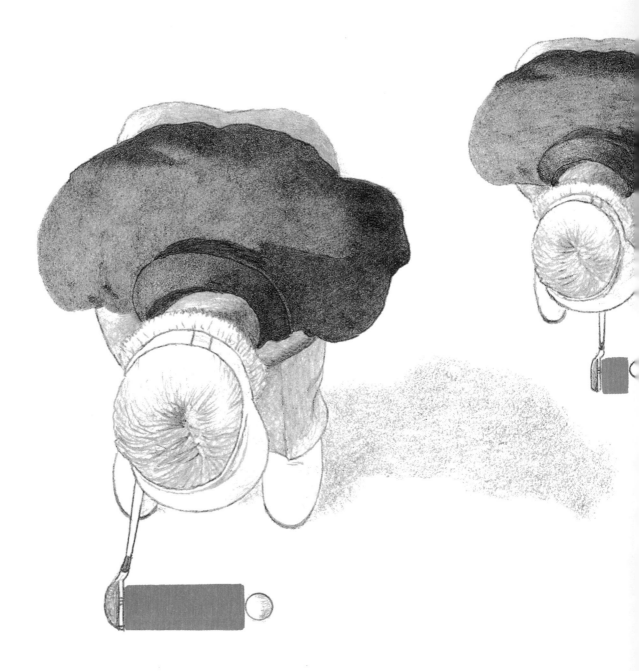

Control Distance with Backswing Length

The more golf I've played, the more convinced I've become that length of backswing, rather than force of strike, should almost always be the controlling factor in rolling the ball the required distance. Which, of course, in its simplest terms, means that the longer the putt, the longer the backswing.

A major reason for this conviction is that I putted my best when I had a sense that the putter was pretty much "swinging itself" at the same general pace of motion on just about every putt I faced, rather than being "forced" to and through the ball in any way.

As putts lengthen, there is obviously a proportional increase in applied hitting force, but in principle I have always wanted the putterhead to swing as freely and naturally as possible as the result of making an appropriately sized backswing.

That's because I've found it awfully difficult—especially in actual tournament play, as opposed to practice—to force the putter in the required direction off a short backswing without upsetting the blade's alignment at impact.

Which, I suspect, is a primary cause of missing "shorties" among recreational players.

Acceleration through Impact a "Must"

As I touched on earlier, coming into the 1967 U.S. Open at Baltusrol it had been an awful year, my longest and worst slump since turning pro, chiefly due to poor putting.

I'd been trying a new putter for some days—that white-painted Bull's Eye lent to me by a friend of a friend referred to earlier—and also was working on a technique variation courtesy of another pal. After watching me miss from all over the practice green for a while, he had suggested I make a shorter backswing in order to produce a more positive hit.

That was the exact opposite of what I'd been practicing for weeks, but it was also how I'd putted well as kid, and, as I also wrote earlier, it helped immediately. I remember that setting up in round two over a crucial 11-footer, I told myself: "Just *believe* in it, will you? Make yourself take it back short, then *hit* it."

> When you're putting badly, it's easy to get so wrapped up in mechanics that you forget the number one fundamental of all golf shots: *Strike the ball.*

The contact that time felt perfect, the ball dropped cleanly, and the huge lift I got produced five more birdies that day and eight more in my final round of 65 to beat Arnold Palmer by four shots and set a then-new Open 72-hole record of 275.

Moral?

When you're putting badly, it's easy to get so wrapped up in mechanics that you forget the number one fundamental of all golf shots: *Strike the ball.* Acceleration through impact is a must, both to reach the hole and keep the ball on line.

Like me on that occasion, you may find the easiest way to ensure that you accelerate through the ball is to shorten your backswing. But, as with any method change, you'll also need some self-pep-talking and extra willpower at first.

"Unweight" but Never "Lift" Club

A putt stroked normally has no spin as it leaves the clubface. Initially the ball skids over the green—the amount depending on the force of hit—before rolling for the remainder of its journey after picking up the momentum of its rotation.

Regardless of that, however, I putt best with a sense—call it an illusion if you like—that I'm starting the ball rolling end over end the moment it leaves the putterface, and to obtain that feeling requires swinging the putter back as close to the ground as possible. This obviously incurs a risk of stubbing the blade, to which my solution is a sense of just barely "unweighting" the putter before starting it back, by raising its head minutely above ground.

However, actually *lifting* the clubhead in initiating the backswing—as I've seen many recreational players do—is a definite no-no, in that it causes a chopping-down or jabbing type of impact that creates backspin and/or sidespin. The other side of the coin is that prematurely lifting the club on the through-stroke promotes a scooping-type action that produces "thin" or semi-topped contact.

Keep Leading Shoulder Low and Still

Another focal point for me in the putting stroke has always been my left shoulder, and especially as a contributor to neither lifting nor twisting the putter blade at the get-go.

As mentioned elsewhere, my wife, Barbara, would often tell me after a poor putting round: "You're lifting your head again!"

Actually, a good part of the time I wasn't.

What sometimes happened was that I unconsciously elevated my left shoulder on the through-swing, which caused my head to rise also.

If you're a congenital head-mover, here's my suggested fix.

As you stroke through the ball, consciously keep your left shoulder *low and still*. Not letting it elevate even the teeniest bit until the putt is on its way will encourage your hands and arms

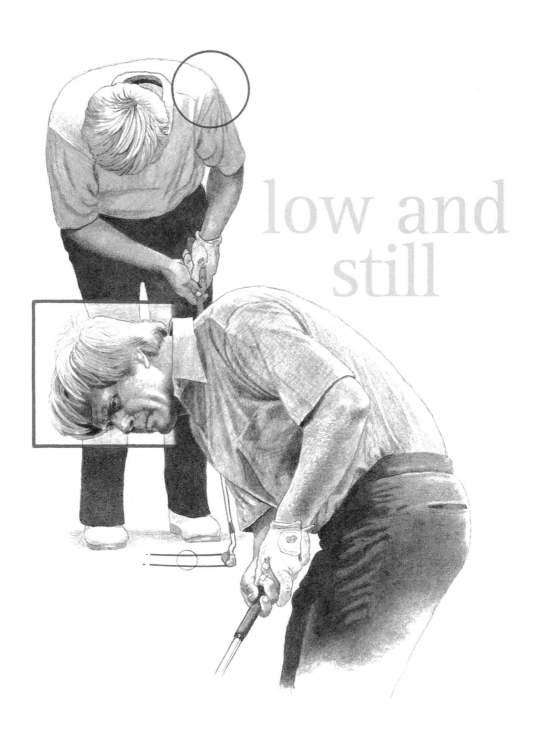

low and
still

to traverse the ball correctly, while also teaching you to follow its roll by swiveling, rather than raising, your head.

This tip, by the way, helped a friend in winning the British Open many years ago after he read it in one of my newspaper features.

Controlling and Checking Face Alignment

Good putting demands squareness of blade and stroke—that is, the putterhead swinging directly along the target line as it moves back from and through the ball with its face looking directly along that line.

One way I've achieved both requirements has been to visualize making the heel of the club travel the same distance as the toe as I mentally rehearse the stroke, then actually see that happen in my peripheral vision as I stroke the ball for real.

One of the most common causes of poor putting is closing the face of the club through the ball, which invariably pulls its entire head to the inside of the target line too quickly. If that's a

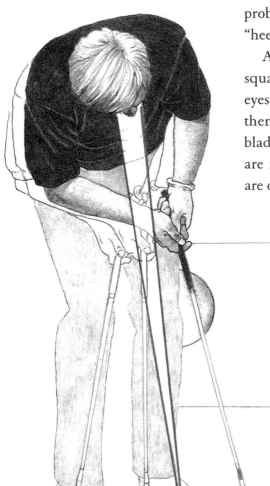

problem for you, I think you'll find my "heel" picture helpful.

An excellent way to check for blade squareness through impact is to fix your eyes on a spot two inches ahead of the ball, then make your normal stroke. The blade's alignment as it passes the area you are focusing on will reveal whether you are opening or closing it.

heel

Look to Your Elbows

Holding my right elbow close to my right side throughout the stroke has always helped me align the putter blade correctly at address, then keep it moving directly along the putt's starting line through impact. I also regard the elbow's "tucked" position as a sort of fulcrum, or guide, in stabilizing my stroke. (Although many golfers putt successfully with the right elbow well clear of their body, care is needed to ensure that it doesn't stray from the side sufficiently to close the putterface and throw the clubhead outside the line in the backswing, resulting in putts being pulled left of target.)

If I'm having difficulty stroking smoothly through the ball, I've found that pointing my left elbow more outward or toward the hole helps me follow through correctly, by encouraging my left hand to keep moving the clubhead cleanly "through" impact. Conversely, if striking the ball solidly is the problem, holding my left elbow closer to my side has sometimes helped me deliver a firmer hit with my right hand.

Experiment in practice to discover which, if any, of these little variations help you stroke better.

Imagine Shaft Is Super Limber

I've done much of my best putting when I've had a distinct sense of gentleness in my hands, in my stroke, and in the way the ball comes off the putterface. In fact, those sensations when perfectly achieved seem to produce so consistent a roll that I've sometimes wondered whether they are the closest thing putting has to a "secret."

Whatever, to promote those feelings, I've found that visualizing the putter shaft as being extremely limber—almost as flexible as a length of rope, in fact—is extremely helpful.

However, if the rope image doesn't seem to be working, I'll sometimes replace it in my mind's eye with that of a delicate glass shaft that will shatter if I'm even a tiny bit harsh through the ball.

In my case, vital to swinging the putter this gently, but with sufficient speed to roll the ball the required distance, is what I

> Visualizing the putter shaft as being extremely limber is extremely helpful.

think of as a positive but "light" grip at address. Equally important is retaining softness in the fingers throughout the stroke—in other words, no involuntary tightening of any part of either hand once the club has been set in motion.

Feel and "See" Deliberate Follow-Through

Just as the follow-through is vital on shots through the green, so it is on putts—and especially those so short you may be inclined either to take them a bit for granted or go at them a little "nervily."

A system that has helped me from time to time to ensure follow-through is to draw an imaginary line along the path I believe the ball will take, then feel and "see" myself carrying the putterface directly along that line for at least three or four inches beyond impact.

Perhaps the greatest benefit in this kind of visualization is guarding against the tendency all of us have from time to time to quit on what we want to think of as "gimmes."

Improve Balance to Stop Body Movement

Pete Egoscue, the anatomical functionalist I've worked with for many years on conditioning myself for both golf and a better quality of life off the course, insists that the ability to achieve and sustain perfect balance is what separates great athletes from merely good ones. He certainly convinced me of the importance of balance in all aspects of golf.

One result was that I was able to help three amateur friends almost miraculously improve their putting. I did this simply by getting them to focus much more heavily on balance by telling them simply one thing: "Set your weight on the balls of your feet."

The most common fault in putting, particularly among amateurs, is moving the body during the stroke. Setting the weight on the balls of the feet makes it harder to move the body, not least because it makes the player more conscious of the need to stay still to sustain perfect balance.

Give it a try any time you're not rolling putts as well as you'd like.

Strike Slightly "Up" to Beat Bumpy Greens

As discussed, putts stroked in the normal way have almost no spin as they leave the clubhead, the ball essentially skidding for a short distance.

When greens are unusually bumpy, this lack of initial spin can become a problem, in that the ball may contact something that deflects it off line before it develops its own inertia. And, of course, that fraction of an inch the ball is knocked off line early can become a matter of feet by the time it reaches the hole.

To help solve that control problem, I suggest you try hitting the ball slightly on the upswing. You'll find that this change in the stroke will give the ball overspin almost from the moment it leaves the clubhead, thereby diminishing the effect of irregularities.

My Five Key Stroking Thoughts

I believe it might be helpful to end this section with a brief review of my stroking basics. Throughout my career, the following have mostly served as my key thoughts as I ready myself to putt:

1   Hold breath just prior to initiating the stroke. By preventing my diaphragm from moving, this helps me keep my head and body perfectly still.

2   Start the putterhead straight back from the ball *smoothly, slowly, and naturally.*

3   Keep the putterhead low to the ground both on the backswing and throughswing.

4   Swing firmly but smoothly through the ball, ensuring that the putterhead never decelerates before impact. Thinking of stroking at a constant speed back and through helps me greatly in avoiding the deadly "decel."

5   Keep the putterface moving along the initial line of the putt for at least three to six inches after the ball is struck, depending on its length.

6

SHORT PUTTS

Two Ways to "Spot Putt"

Over the years, I've only occasionally "spot putted,"
a technique where you pick a mark on the green
between your ball and the cup as an aiming point.
My preference is usually to visualize the overall line in
my mind's eye. On occasion, however, spot putting
has helped me, especially with the shorties, as it might
also you.

There are two spot-putting techniques that I've tried. The first involves identifying then aiming at a mark on the green just a few inches ahead of your ball on the line that you have decided will take it to the hole. The second method is to pick a spot a few inches short of the hole to roll the ball over. Try both techniques and consider using whichever one works best for you.

Committed spot putters claim that aiming for a point much smaller than a 4¼-inch hole helps them roll the ball with greater accuracy. Other proponents say it helps in becoming less fixated on the hole, encouraging them to make freer, more relaxed strokes.

Either way, it's worth a try, especially if you're not dropping many putts when aiming less specifically.

Identify then aim at a mark on the green just a few inches ahead of your ball on the line that you have decided will take it to the hole.

spot putt

Fitting Speed to Slope

My routine way of handling short breaking downhill putts has mostly been to "die" the ball gently into the front of the hole after a careful computation of break and speed. Prompting caution, of course, is that the more downhill the putt, the less the cup's lowered rear area serves as a backstop.

However, I will never forget one great exception to that approach.

If my first major championship win as a pro, the 1962 U.S. Open at Oakmont, hinged on any one shot, it was a 4-foot putt that, had I not made it for a par on the 71st hole, there would have been no playoff with Arnold Palmer.

The putt was an extremely difficult one, with a break first to the right and then to the left, and in holing it I taught myself a lesson that has stayed with me ever since. That is, the greater pressure you are under, the better off you are playing boldly rather than cautiously on "must" short putts.

Deciding that I had neither the nerve nor the delicacy at that stage of the proceedings either to read or play a soft double-breaking putt, I chose to rap the ball firmly enough to negate most of them. In fact, I hit the ball so hard that Bob Jones, watching on TV, later wrote me, "When I saw the ball dive into the hole, I almost jumped right out of my chair."

This be-firm-under-pressure policy has worked for me chiefly, I'm sure, because it's in sync with the aggressive instinct one inevitably feels when the adrenaline is pumping. Also, "dying" the ball into the cup on a short breaking putt requires that you perfectly judge both speed and direction, whereas by going more boldly for the hole you eliminate or reduce the subtleties involved.

the time to be bold

For that reason, especially when I'm stroking the ball well, I almost always have tried to "firm" rather than "finesse" breaking uphill putts straight into the hole or at least counter as much of the break as possible with speed of roll. In that regard, the fact that the raised rear portion of the cup offers more of a backstop than on a level putt also offers encouragement to be bold.

I made my putter grips so short I could hold them only near the top.

Don't Choke Down

All of us tend to become a bit tentative on the little ones at times, which frequently has the effect of causing clubhead deceleration before impact—a guaranteed way to leave the ball short or wide of the hole or both.

In that regard, I advise against choking down on the club on short putts. That's because doing so makes the club feel lighter than usual, which tends to promote a different quality of stroke—usually a more tentative or jerky one. To be sure that didn't happen to me, I made my putter grips so short I could hold them only near the top.

Also, to ensure that you strike the ball firmly enough, try making an exaggerated follow-through by swinging the putterhead six to nine inches directly along the line of the putt past the hole without letting its face open or close.

A little practice doing this on 3- and 4-footers and you should quickly gain the feel of accelerating through the ball—not to mention that nice solid sensation of striking it with a truly square clubface.

7

LONG PUTTS

Make Certainty of "Read" Mandatory

Frequently in pro-ams over the years, an amateur partner would walk up and hit a really long putt after no more than a cursory glance at the terrain he had to cover. Then he would whine when the ball finished many feet short, long, or wide of the hole.

Putting after only a casual glance at what lies between your ball and the cup may be okay if you are out just getting exercise, but it's a very bad habit to get into if you're ever going to play golf to the best of your ability.

That's because, the longer the putt, the greater the chance it will involve multiple breaks, and wet or dry spots, and variations in grass length or density, and challenging grain patterns. All such conditions—and also strong wind—will affect the ball's behavior, which is one reason I almost always walked off very long putts, as well as assessing them from behind the ball, and generally also from sideways on.

Pacing the distance on a very long putt also often helped me develop a feel for the "weight" of the stroke I would need to get the ball to the hole.

Whatever it took, the tougher the putt, the harder I worked at the "read," with absolute certainty about what I would be attempting to do being mandatory before I stroked.

Putting after just a casual glance at what lies between your ball and the cup is a very bad habit to get into if you're ever going to play golf to the best of your ability.

"read"

Speed of Roll Always Top Priority

If you have trouble getting very long putts close despite working hard at reads, it's probably time to check your stroking technique.

Your objective is to find and hone a stroke that enables you to consistently strike the ball the correct distance. As stressed throughout this book, I believe that is most easily achieved when I have a sense of the club virtually "swinging itself," rather than being forced or hurried in any way.

Indeed, trying to force the putterhead to swing harder or faster than your ideal pace on long putts is a sure way to misalign both its face and path at impact. If you suspect you are doing either or both those things, take yourself off to the practice green and try controlling distance primarily through the length of your back- and through-swings, rather than the force of the hit.

As I also stress repeatedly herein, the tempo of my stroke is always more important than its mechanics in achieving that goal. Accordingly, I try to swing the putterhead at more or less the same pace on all putts. Try making that your primary practice and playing objective, too.

Also, in "reading" long putts, be sure you pay sufficient attention to speed as well as line. Study your playing partners and I'm sure you'll notice that they stroke many more long putts either well short of or way past the hole than they badly misdirect the ball.

That's because most people can intuitively "see" or sense the line of a putt better than they can compute, memorize, and control its "weight." In which situation, of course the longer the putt, the more vital it becomes to putt with speed rather than direction at the forefront of your mind.

Mastering "Monsters"

Early in my career, very long putts gave me more trouble than they should have done.

Here are four tactics that eventually helped me, and might help you also, with the "monsters."

First, improve your sense of the "weight" of stroke needed by walking all the way from the ball to the hole and back—including even pacing off the distance if you think knowing it in approximate yardage might help.

Second, take the most upright stance over the ball that you comfortably can, making it just that little bit easier to see the entire landscape between you and the hole, and thus better judge the distance, right up to the moment of stroking. This minor but important adjustment should also help you swing the putter more fully and freely.

Third, concentrate more on solid contact with the ball than on pinpoint accuracy of line, because you are much more likely to be ten feet short or long of the hole than ten feet right or left on very long putts.

Fourth—and most important in my case—seek to strongly visualize a circle around the hole about 6 feet in diameter, into which you will attempt to "die" the ball, leaving you with no more than a 3-footer.

Finally, don't be too greedy. From 50 feet or more, recognize that even a great putter is doing well to consistently get within 3 feet of the hole. So make that your goal, not the cup itself.

visualize

3'

Double-Breaker Strategy

As previously noted, occasionally on short putts I will use a spot on the intended line as a target, but on long ones I invariably prefer to work with an overall "mind picture" of the line the ball must travel.

However, where I've found putting to a particular mark or small area of green helpful is on severely double-breaking putts.

Here's the technique.

Study each break separately until you can identify the point at which you believe the second break will take effect. Then, in stroking, concentrate on getting the ball to that point by playing it to take the first break only.

Obviously, with this method you also need to have programmed a "weight" of stroke that will roll the ball the required distance.

> Where I've found putting to a particular mark or small area of green helpful is on severely double-breaking putts.

Strengthening Depth Perception

Some tour players like the flagstick removed on all putts where they can clearly see the hole, but I've always preferred it to be attended on putts of 25 feet or more.

Reason?

Having the pin in the cup strengthens my depth perception, thereby more clearly identifying the target location during those final crucial assessments of and decisions about speed and line as I set up over the ball.

8

PRACTICE

Work on Putts That Matter Most

Watching amateurs practice before pro-ams, I've often noticed them putting mostly from long range and wondered accordingly how many such monsters they expect to hole on the course.

Hitting a few roller-coasters is good for figuring the overall pace of the greens and for developing a fluid

12'

stroking motion. But from about 15 feet in is where you most need accuracy and confidence in terms of scoring well.

Also, never neglect those 3- and 4-footers if you'd like less pressure on your chips and long putts. In fact, watch the tour pros warm up and you'll invariably see them working on "shorties" as their final warm-up activity before teeing off in tournament rounds.

If you really get desperate over the tiddlers, try the age-old trick of practicing from 3 or 4 feet to a tee stuck in the ground rather than to a hole. By making you less "cup conscious," this will allow you to concentrate harder first on critical setup factors, then on your stroke mechanics and tempo.

Also, once you get on the course, the hole should look like a bucket!

My Four Practice Systems

I practiced putting in my peak years essentially in four ways.

When my stroke went sour, I worked on it by hitting balls with very little concern for where they went. Of primary importance was tempo and solid contact. Once I had hit, say, ten putts consecutively at the tempo and with the contact feel I was seeking between my hands and the clubface, I quit. That's because I knew I couldn't "mechanize" or "groove" the action forever and that by going on longer I could lose whatever touch I'd just developed. Thus I always stopped when I felt I had fully achieved my objective, even though I knew my success may only be temporary.

My second form of putting practice throughout my best years consisted of fairly frequent but relatively short sessions when I was at home, basically checking out and tuning my grip, setup, stroke, tempo, etc. Whether I holed a lot of putts during those sessions was much less important to me than developing good feelings about those factors.

During my peak years, I did my third type of putting practice before each tournament round. Then, I would stroke the ball to a definite target, but with the prime objective of relating the tempo and mechanics of the stroke to the conditions I would find on the golf course—what you might call "feeling out" the greens as they were that day, and also my metabolism of the moment and trying to harmonize the two. At some point, I would stroke a few really long putts to measure how well I was judging distance. Most of the time, though, I worked from about 15 feet down to about 4 feet—the "makeable" putt range.

Such sessions rarely lasted more than ten to fifteen minutes, because I would quit as soon as I felt I'd matched my stroke to the speed or texture of the greens, even if I'd only been out there briefly by the standards of other players. That was because I have never believed in wasting putts on practice greens.

My fourth type of practice happened on the golf course itself. In making practice swings with the putter, I never just waved it around in order to ease my nerves or kill time. With each practice stroke I tried to simulate the exact feel of the upcoming putt in terms of rhythm and length of swing. In short, I simultaneously measured and rehearsed the real thing through my very deliberate practice swings.

You might find that such a positive attitude on practice strokes greatly boosts your ability to concentrate as well as your physical abilities.

If you've never had a set plan for putting practice, I recommend the above to you wholeheartedly— especially the fourth aspect of it. You might find that such a positive attitude on practice strokes greatly boosts your ability to concentrate as well as your physical abilities.

Five More Get-Better Pointers

Here are five more pointers on putting practice that you might find helpful if you don't already employ them.

First, avoid practicing too much on any one type of green or any one type of putt. Even on the same course, greens vary from day to day or even hour to hour, and you need to be able to handle the variations. So switch your practice locations and angles as much as possible.

Second, remember that distance always is more difficult to judge than direction in putting. So always practice speed more than accuracy.

Third, instead of practicing to an actual hole, try putting to a tee stuck in the ground. By making you less "cup conscious," putting to such a tiny target will help you concentrate better on speed and line, and thus on tempo and stroke pattern.

Four, startling as the thought may be, recognize that quantity of practice alone will not make you a good putter. What I mean is that you cannot become a good putter by going out on the practice green every day and hitting a hundred or more balls at the hole. That's because putting is strictly a matter of feel, touch, and timing, and thus working to improve those three qualities should always be your priority in practice. Go beyond that point and you will become what I call "mechanized" and risk losing your sense of touch. So practice until you feel you are putting well, then stop while your confidence remains high.

Fifth, stress practicing the putts you can reasonably expect to make. Lagging a few long putts during every session is valuable in judging distance, and it will help with the tempo of your stroke. But it's on putts from 15 feet or less that you are always looking to hole out. And that is where practice will pay the greatest dividends.

9

FAULTS AND FIXES

Making More
"Shorties," 1

As we touched on earlier, following poor short-putting rounds, my wife, Barbara, must have told me a thousand times, "You're moving your head again!"—and some of the time she was right.

I suppose it's just an instinctive part of the human make-up that, the more critical putting well is to succeeding at golf, the quicker we want to watch the ball roll—which, of course, is the primary cause of premature head and upper body movement.

I've tried many ways to win this battle with myself over the years, but the one that seems to have worked best is possibly the simplest.

It consists of reminding myself, just before stroking, not to allow any head or upper body movement before the ball has traveled at least 3 or 4 feet. A more severe variation is to forcefully will myself to keep my head and torso where I put them at address until the ball either stops or drops.

Focus and self-discipline are the most critical factors in staying still over short putts.

Another factor we touched on earlier can also be very helpful in avoiding the dreaded forward head or body shift—that being to keep one's left shoulder as still and low as possible while stroking through the ball.

In the end, though, focus and self-discipline are the most critical factors in staying still over short putts.

Making More "Shorties," 2

Another common cause of missing short putts is taking too long a backswing, which can then cause you instinctively to both decelerate the putterhead and distort its face alignment on the throughswing.

One way to work on fixing this is to practice with a blocking object—a tee peg will do—stuck in the green 2 to 3 inches behind the putterhead, thereby forcing you to shorten your backswing. The resulting sense of exaggerating your follow-through will then help you accelerate the putterhead through, not just to, the ball.

If that doesn't solve the problem, try the exact opposite by swinging the putterhead in practice twice as far back as you have been doing, then commensurately more easily to and through the ball.

If you're like me, you'll find letting the putterhead do most of the work has a distinct smoothing effect on your stroking action—not to mention your nervous system!

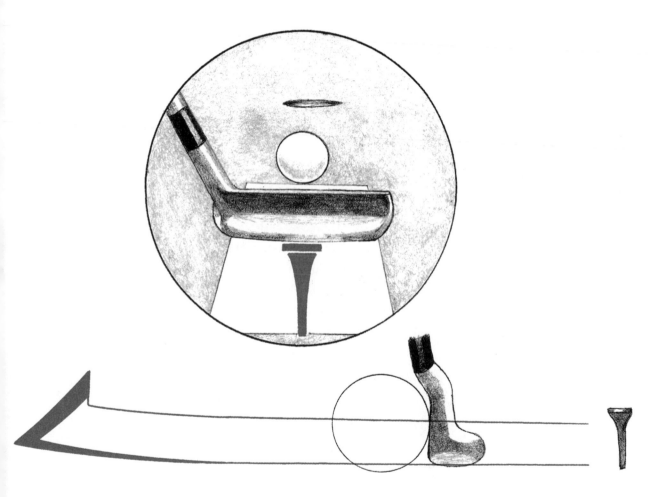

Beating the "Yips"

"Yipping" putts is probably golf's worst affliction, and often infuriatingly difficult to overcome. That's because they represent a vicious circle—the more you "yip," the less your brain's negative impact on your nervous system will let you do otherwise.

Like so many golfers so afflicted, a friend of mine was making a short, quick backstroke, then sort of desperately flicking at the ball with his hands. Those moves distorted both the putterhead's path and its alignment at impact.

To overcome those faults and begin his recovery, I had him set the putter handle firmly against the palm or thumb pad of his left hand, rather than in the fingers. Next, I told him to focus on swinging the grip end of the putter rather than its head—to the point of not even looking at the clubhead as he practiced stroking putts.

Finally, I suggested that he work on swinging the putterhead back 1 inch for every foot of green he needed to roll the ball and to follow through the same distance. For instance, on a 3-footer, the putterhead would move 3 inches back from the

ball, then 3 inches past the point of impact. This served to lengthen and further smooth his stroke, eventually eliminating any remaining tendency to jerk the putter back, then jab at the ball.

If you're a "yipper," try these simple exercises, because, as they did for my friend, they should help you regain your form on the greens—and your sanity!

Try More Backswing, Not Force

Attempting to roll the ball the desired distance by forcing the putterhead to swing shorter but faster than your normal tempo of stroking on long putts is a sure way to misalign its path and face, especially by upsetting the rhythm of your action.

Much better is to control the amount of roll by adjusting the length of your backswing.

I have always tried to swing the putterhead at pretty much the same pace on all putts—the ideal in my case being a sense of the clubhead virtually "swinging itself."

Distance is then varied simply by increasing or decreasing my length of backswing.

Ensuring Square-Bladed Impact

Unknowingly striking the ball with the clubface open or closed to the desired starting line is a frequent cause of poor greens work.

Here's a way to check whether you are doing that.

After lining up, fix your eyes on a spot about 2 inches ahead of the ball, then stroke normally. The angle of the blade as it travels through your area of vision will reveal its alignment at impact.

If misalignment shows up, here's a practice tip to help you fix the problem.

Mark a chalk line along the starting path of some practice putts, then try to carry the putter blade straight along that line after impact for at least 5 or 6 inches.

A bonus of this drill is that you will stroke the ball more firmly, as well as squarely, by accelerating through it better.

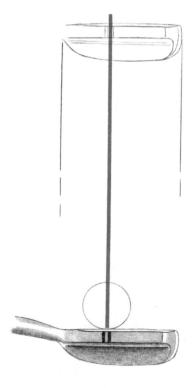

A Couple of "Pulling" Cures

Do you tend to miss a lot of putts—and especially shorties—by pulling them?

If so, try setting your left hand on the club with its back looking a little more to the left of the target.

Gripping thus, you will be less likely to rotate your hands to the left as you stroke through the ball.

Also, setting your left thumb firmly along the top of the shaft, then using it as the fulcrum or pivot of the stroke, often helps in keeping the blade square through impact.

10

STRATEGY

Know the Rules

I imagine most golfers think of the *Rules of Golf* as chiefly penalizing, but the fact is that thorough knowledge of them can sometimes save strokes—both through the green and on it—as in the following putting situation.

It's rained, you get to the green, and a puddle of water lies between your ball and the hole. What to do?

The first part of the answer lies in the "Definition" of "Abnormal Ground Conditions" in the *Rules of Golf*, which reads as follows: "An 'abnormal ground condition' is any casual water, ground under repair or hole, cast or runway on the course made by a burrowing animal, a reptile or a bird."

Rule 25, covering what action to take in the event of such conditions (and other factors), supplies the second part:

rule 25 If the ball lies on the putting green, the player must lift the ball and place it without penalty at the nearest point of relief that is not in a hazard, or if complete relief is impossible, at the nearest point to where it lay that affords maximum available relief from the condition, but not nearer the hole and not in a hazard. The nearest point of relief or maximum relief available relief may be off the putting green.

The constantly updated *Rules of Golf* is available from the U.S. Golf Association, Liberty Corner Road, P.O. Box 708, Far Hills, NJ 07931; phone: (908) 234-2300; fax: (908) 234-9687; Web site: www.rulesofgolf.com. If you haven't already, I suggest you get a copy and study it.

If in Doubt, Always Check

If you encounter a situation, especially in tournament play, where you don't know or are uncertain about how to proceed under the rules, never be afraid to check before playing your next shot.

Here's my prime personal example of how costly that can be.

Still an amateur, I was leading the 1960 U.S. Open by a stroke on the 67th hole at Cherry Hills. I hit a 3-wood and 9-iron 12 feet from the pin. My partner, going for a fifth Open victory and at that point just two shots back of me, was the great Ben Hogan.

Overly "pumped," I stroked my putt a little too hard and it rolled 18 inches past the cup. Studying the shortie, I noticed there was a small indentation, left by a poorly repaired pitch mark, dead between my ball and the hole.

Excited, anxious, under as much pressure as I had ever experienced, I failed to focus clearly on whether the rules allowed me to repair the ball mark (they did). Too shy or embarrassed to admit this in front of Hogan, with whom I was playing for the first time, or to hold up play at that late stage in the national championship by asking for an official ruling, I stroked the putt. The mark deflected the ball just enough to spin it out.

Upset, I three-putted the next green, and Arnie Palmer, with his phenomenal historic charge, won the title with me second, two strokes back.

Moral?

Again, if in doubt—especially when it really matters—never be afraid to check.

Club Yourself with Putting in Mind

If your game is being hurt by poor long putting, give consideration to your approach club selection as well as to your greens work.

I remember a green at home in the States when I was playing the tour regularly that was some 80 yards long, and another that called for a 4-iron to a front pin position and a 3-wood to a cup cut near the back. Under certain conditions, such discrepancies are particularly common on the Old Course's huge

double greens in British Opens played at St. Andrews.

Obviously, poor approach club selection in such instances is bound to result in way too many three-putts.

Incidentally, I have found that, on a strange course, you can learn a lot about green sizes and approach shot distances by relating to the size of the players in the groups ahead of you.

Chip or Putt from Off the Green?

Whether to chip or putt from the fringe of the green depends mostly on your confidence level in each type of shot.

Generally, I would recommend putting, for two reasons.

The first is that way back in my earliest pro days, after watching me chip poorly from just off a green, Arnold Palmer told me, "I've found over the years that my worst putt from the fringe is at least as good as my best chip. Or, in other words, if you get the ball to, say, only within five feet of the hole from fifty feet with the putter, that's about as bad as you'll do. But you've got to hit a darn good chip from fifty feet to get the ball closer than that to the hole."

The advice was typical of Arn's helpful approach to me as a tour rookie, and I quickly discovered that it was true for me too, and so stuck with it from then on.

> Arnold Palmer told me, "I've found over the years that my worst putt from the fringe is at least as good as my best chip."

The second reason I mostly favor the putter is that, over time as a golfer, you putt so much more than you chip that the odds must surely make you almost certain to perform better with the flat stick.

I particularly favor putting—anywhere from a few feet to as much as 30 yards off the green—when the lie is good, the fairway grass is relatively smooth, and the grain runs toward the hole. However, the longer the grass the ball sits in and the more breaks ands/or bumps it will encounter, the more likely I am to chip.

Get Help When a Problem Becomes Severe

One reason I spent so much time during my peak playing career with my friend and original teacher, Jack Grout, is that it was much more difficult than it is today for a player to be able to see himself in action on film or videotape. That being the case, you might think you knew what you were doing wrong, but were usually guessing and consequently often wrongly.

Also, when a problem in any aspect of golf becomes really persistent and severe, it's awfully easy to overexperiment yourself into even greater trouble. To avoid that, and to save time, my answer was always to enlist Jack's eagle eye and great knowledge of my methods—most of them taught by him during my teens. And if I had it all to do over again, that would still be my system.

But there was one memorable instance where television did the job for me.

My problem was eye alignment at address with the putter.

As covered earlier, one of my few hard and fast rules about putting is to set up with your eyes directly over the ball, and thereby directly over the line along which you need to start the ball.

Fail to do that, and, if your eyes are "inside" the ball, you'll tend to aim the putter face right of the correct line. In this instance, I was doing the opposite: eyes out beyond the ball, making me aim the putterface to the left of the line I'd identified when reading the putt from directly behind the ball.

The event was the 1966 Masters, and I'd tied with Gay Brewer and Tommy Jacobs after 72 holes, despite my putting ranging from average to awful all week. I was just about to go work on it again when I saw myself on a CBS replay not even

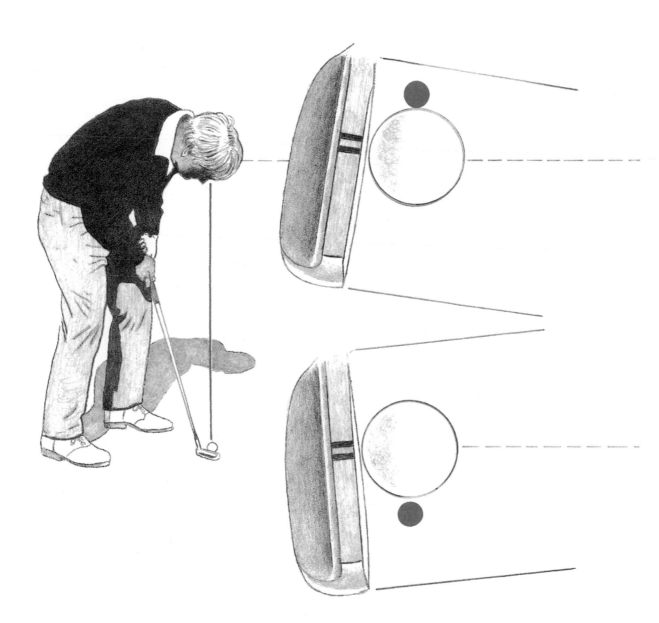

touching the hole from 3½ feet for a birdie at the 17th—the miss that had cost me outright victory.

Well, I virtually jogged to the practice green, where, as soon as I repositioned my eyes directly over the ball, everything fell into place.

I did not hit one bad putt the next day, and by its end had become the first man to help himself into a green jacket by winning back-to-back Masters.

Listen to a Knowledgeable Caddie

Here's one more example of the importance of making up one's mind in "reading" putts.

It's the 1980 PGA Championship at Oak Hill, and on the ninth hole of the final round I sense that making or missing a very slick downhill, sidehill 12-footer for birdie might be the difference between winning and losing my fifth victory in the year's last major.

As I'm finally figuring that the ball will break about 5 inches to the left, my son Jackie, who's caddying for me, says, "Dad, I think it's going to go slightly left to right." That starts me rereading and rethinking the putt, and suddenly I find what Jackie is seeing. The putt does not break as much to the left as I originally figured. Playing accordingly, I make it.

The moral?

Vagueness or doubt about line almost guarantees poor putting in that it produces sloppy blade alignment at address, a sense of which then prevents a positive, fully committed stroke.

Accordingly, especially when I have a caddie who can supply an informed second opinion, I take full advantage of it. My sons know golf, and my game particularly, and they also have great "eyes," so I've always listened when I thought they had something to contribute when caddying for me.

Most of all, though, never play a stroke with doubt in your mind. With or without help, make your decision clearly and firmly, then be positive with the putt.

With or without help, make your decision clearly and firmly, then be positive with the putt.

"Read" Every Factor
Every Time . . .

Reading greens is an art form that requires both knowledge and effort.

For instance, in addition to contouring, almost all types of greens possess some degree of grain, but an awful lot of makeable putts are missed by recreational golfers who either don't notice it or don't know how to read it. Other commonly neglected factors include moisture, wind, and time of day.

Let's discuss grain first.

Most grasses grow either toward the nearest water source or in the direction of drainage, although in some parts of the world, certain strains—including most Bermudas—grow predominantly toward the setting sun. Your best visual indicator of grain direction is the sheen of the grass.

If the surface looks light or silvery as you assess a putt, you are generally putting down grain, in which case the ball will roll faster and break more. Conversely, when the surface appears dark, dirty, or matte-looking, you are stroking into the grain, meaning the ball will roll more slowly and break less.

Putting across the grain, of course, influences both speed and break, and especially as the ball slows.

Turning to moisture, you should recognize that there are two types of wet greens. When moisture has really soaked into the ground, you can be sure that a putt will almost invariably roll slower and break less than normal, thus necessitating an appropriate "read" along with firmer stroking. Conversely, when greens are only lightly filmed with moisture, as with morning dew or after a brief shower, generally they will play only slightly slower than normal, calling for almost the same weight of "strike" as on dry surfaces.

moisture

Regarding wind, a mild breeze usually will affect the ball's roll little or not at all except possibly on super-fast greens, whereas a strong blow most definitely will, particularly as the ball slows down.

wind

As for time of day, and especially in good weather, remember that the grass is growing as you play, and that the greens therefore will become a little slower—and grainier—over your final holes.

. . . But Prioritize Speed Control

As just mentioned, because my sons have all been good players with excellent vision, I conferred with them on putts when they carried the bag for me. Otherwise, I preferred to read the greens by myself.

Why?

Because the line of every putt depends on the speed at which the ball is rolled, and since the player alone controls speed through the force of the stroke, only he or she can determine how much break to play.

It takes both practice and experience to figure out how effort relates to distance, but this should be your primary objective on all middle- to long-range putts. Analyze where you usually miss such putts, and I'm sure you'll find you misjudge distance more than direction. In fact, I believe most amateurs would do well to work on speed control over anything else when their putting goes sour.

It's also important to have a realistic approach to putting. We all love to make long putts, but my objective from more than 12 to 15 feet out—and particularly under pressure—is to leave myself a tap-in when the ball doesn't drop, which is most of the time.

As a reminder, to help me gauge speed on most long putts, I focus on rolling the ball at a pace that will put it within a 3-foot circle around the hole.

Haven't missed many of those 18-inchers over the years!

To help me gauge speed on most long putts, I focus on rolling the ball at a pace that will put it within a 3-foot circle around the hole.

My Pre-Stroking Routine

All good golfers develop a set of routines that best enable them to prepare properly for all types of shots.

Here's mine on the putting green.

First, as I walk up to and onto the green, I size up the surrounding terrain, and especially on hilly courses, because knowing the overall contours of the land will help me determine both line and speed. By that I mean most putts will more likely turn with the general or primary slope of the green than against it.

Second, I check overall slopes and contours of the green, the grain direction, the length, texture, and quality of the grass, and any moisture and wind factors.

Next, I assess the specific angles between ball and cup, mostly from directly behind the ball and in a squatting position or bent over from the waist. That's because, if you stand erect in assessing the line, the more subtle undulations in the green will tend to flatten out. Conversely, if you were to lie on your belly, all you would see would be the ups and downs in the immediate foreground.

Especially on less than perfect greens and/or long, multi-breaking putts, I most carefully evaluate the area immediately around the hole. What I'm mostly looking for are surface irregularities that could affect the ball's behavior as it loses momentum—it being a basic of putting that the slower the ball rolls, the more it breaks with whatever slope it encounters, and/or is deflected by any irregularities it meets.

If a fellow player must putt before I do, I watch carefully how his ball behaves in terms of speed and break, and particularly if his line is anything like mine. (I'm careful in all of this not to take so much time I hold up play, which is easiest if you can do your surveying while others are doing theirs.)

As I step up to the ball, I compute all of the factors I've evaluated into a complete mental picture of what I must do to get the ball into or very close to the cup.

At that point I make a couple of practice swings from behind the ball, trying exactly to reproduce the stroke I've decided I need.

Next, I make whatever slight adjustments I figure are necessary to my stance and other bodily positions as I glance a time or two at the line of the putt by looking past—but never by raising my head over—my left shoulder.

Almost ready now, I hold my breath as I try to "see" the ball in my mind's-eye either dropping or stopping within tap-in distance of the hole.

Finally, I stroke only when I feel one hundred percent "ready."

Finally, I stroke only when I feel one hundred percent "ready."

"See" Distances Incrementally

Some golfers try to compute speed on a long putt simply by obtaining a general impression of the terrain between the ball and the cup. Others will survey the territory from all angles or actually pace off the distance as they examine the line.

Depending on the difficulty of the putt, I'll do some or all of those things. Over the years, however, I found that mentally visualizing the distance in 5- to 10-foot increments as I stood behind the ball generally gave me the best sense of how forcefully I needed to stroke.

Give that a try if you tend to roll the ball either long or short, particularly on exceptionally long putts.

Four Tips to Tame a Brute

The tougher a putt is to read, and especially long downhillers, the more carefully you should identify the ball's starting line, then commit to it totally at address with your blade and body alignment.

Fail to do that and you are likely to try to reroute the putt with your stroke, which invariably is costly.

Next, remember that you'll retain smoothness and good tempo by swinging longer rather than by hitting harder—by which I mean not trying to force the distance, especially when your nerves may be jumping a little.

Third, you'll improve your chances by carefully rehearsing the longer stroke deliberately a number of times and calming any "butterflies" by taking some deep breaths while you do so.

> Remember that you'll retain smoothness and good tempo by swinging longer rather than by hitting harder.

Defanging
Downhillers

Most recreational golfers miss tricky downhill putts, especially on super-fast greens, because their fear of them breeds hesitant stroking.

How I've taken much of the anxiety out of such shots is to forget about the slope and play the putt as though it were on level ground.

For example, if a downhiller was actually 10 feet but would reach the hole with only the force needed for a 3-footer on level turf, I would aim at a point 3 feet away and stroke for that distance.

The effect was that the more precise feel and greater confidence I had for a putt of that length allowed me to make a more positive stroke. I think that will happen in your case also.

Spin Ball Sooner on Poor Greens

Let me remind you that, even when stroked perfectly, a golf ball always skids a little before it begins rolling perfectly, the distance of the skid depending on the force of the hit determined by the length of the putt.

On bumpy or spiked-up greens, the tendency for the ball to be deflected by an irregularity is greater while it's totally or partially skidding than after it has developed sufficient momentum to roll truly end over end. And of course, the earlier the ball is knocked off line, the bigger the directional error at the end of its journey.

Although a more lofted putter will help to minimize skidding, physics dictate that there is no total antidote to this problem. However, a partial solution used by many tour pros, myself included, is to start the ball rolling as early as possible by positioning it

Even when stroked perfectly, a golf ball always skids a little before it begins rolling perfectly.

a little more forward at address, then striking it just past the bottom of the putterhead's arc or slightly on the upswing.

Give this technique a try the next time the greens are not up to par.

When Putting Uphill
Is Best

Have trouble on extremely fast greens? Here's a tip that will help you.

In assessing distance and force of stroke, plan if possible to leave yourself an uphill putt should you not hole the first one.

On very slick greens I'd rather have even a side-hill short putt than one going straight down a pronounced slope, because those "sliders" are the trickiest in the game both to assess and stroke.

So good strategy on slick surfaces involves careful planning slope-wise, especially on long approach putts.

Incidentally, the same advice applies to chip shots.

Putting from Bunkers

Putting out of a bunker can be a good percentage shot, provided the trap is relatively flat with little or no overhanging lip and its sand is sufficiently firm.

I do everything as normal in such circumstances, with the exception of hitting the ball off the toe rather than the center of the putter blade.

That's because this form of impact tends to impart what I think of as a more "slinging" action to the ball, allowing it to roll more freely by reducing backspin.

Forget Unnecessary
Heroics . . .

In match play especially, never try to be a hero on the greens when there is no need for heroics.

For instance, if your opponent is 20 feet away and you 40 feet, work at lagging your putt "dead" rather than risking three-putting by trying to hole it.

The percentages are that both of you will miss your first putts. If that happens and you three-putt, but the other person gets down in two, you will feel that you've given away the hole and risk getting down on yourself as a result.

Should your opponent hole out, then he's simply beaten some pretty long odds, and you have nothing to berate yourself about.

. . . But Know When to Go for Broke

It's the 1975 Masters, the final round, the par-3 16th hole, and I'm battling Tom Weiskopf and Johnny Miller, who are playing immediately behind me.

Tom Watson, my playing partner, after finding water from the tee, hits his second tee shot on the green a little farther from the hole than my 40-footer, but on much the same line, so will putt first.

The pin is cut scarily near the front of the small plateau at the back right corner of the green. I watch the roll of Tom's ball very carefully, as one always should in such situations.

Nevertheless, examining the line from behind my ball, I'm still thinking, "Make par and go on your way." Then, straightening up after one last look, I realize I can "see" the line in my mind's eye about as clearly as I ever have on a putt of such length. Immediately, my thought as I complete my setup becomes, "Make it!"

"see"

I stroke the ball solidly and dead on the intended line. As it gets within about a dozen feet of the cup, I just know there's no way it can miss and I lift my putter high overhead. As the ball drops, both my caddie and I turn into Indian war dancers. Half an hour later, I've won a then-record fifth Masters.

Moral?

Trust your senses whenever you're "seeing" putting lines well and stroking the ball solidly. You aren't ever going to make a lot of 40-footers, but when both line and speed get into perfect mind's-eye focus, go ahead and go for broke.

CONCLUSION

·

MY PUTTING "MUSTS"

I think it would be appropriate to conclude this book with a short list of my absolute "musts" for good putting, as developed throughout my career. Having tried so many variations over the years, it took a bit of thought, but here's what I finally came up with:

- Having the knowledge—and patience—to correctly "read" greens.
- Understanding that speed always determines line.
- Being comfortable at address by achieving good balance.
- Setting one's eyes directly over the starting line of the putt, so that the brain can "see" it accurately.
- Controlling the stroke with the wrists and arms.
- Ensuring that the leading hand guides the stroke, while the trailing hand delivers the hit.
- Having the putter shaft aligned vertically at both address and impact.
- Keeping the putterhead low to the ground both back and through.
- Continuing the follow-through along the target line.
- Keeping the head and body still throughout the stroke.
- Most critical of all: having a positive attitude. Believe you can make 'em and you frequently will. Believe you can't and you generally won't.

I wish everyone who reads this book as much good fortune on the greens as I enjoyed over so many years of playing the greatest game of all.